KU-496-667

2 elephants

3 pigs

My Animal
COUNTING

Illustrated by Mary Lonsdale

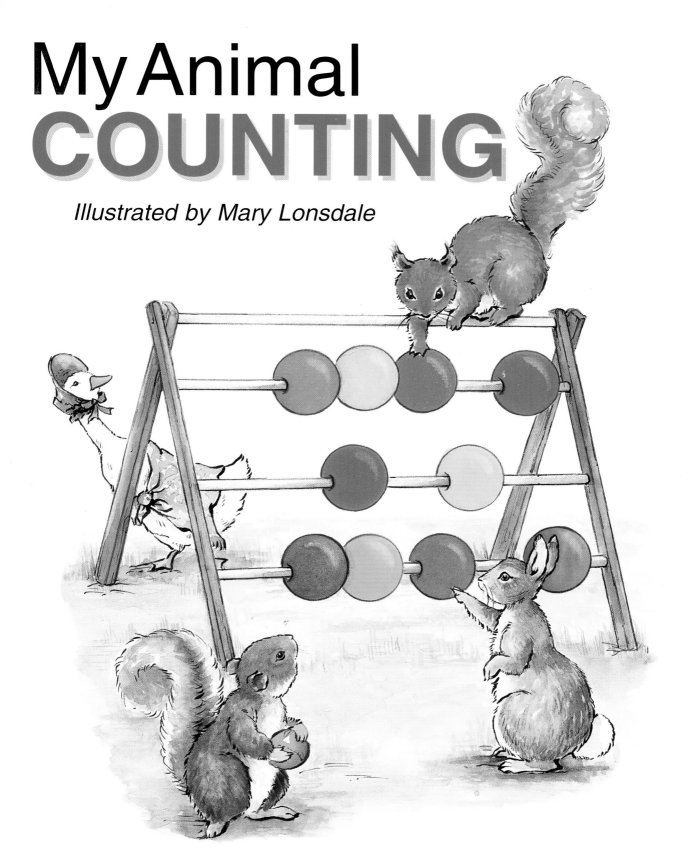

AWARD PUBLICATIONS LIMITED

1 dog

4 hippos

5 birds

6 monkeys

7 foxes

8 mice

9 lambs

10 bears

11 ducks

12 rabbits

2 kittens

4 butterflies

6 rabbits

7 carrots

8 sheep

1 sheepdog

1 cow

2 calves

5 geese

8 goose eggs

5 hens

10 chicks

1 bear

12 honey-bees

3 otters

3 fish

9 frogs

4 water lilies

4 dragonflies

8 fish

1 owl

12 pine cones

8 red squirrels

11 acorns

ISBN 0-86163-944-8

Copyright © 1998 Award Publications Limited

Published by Award Publications Limited,
1st Floor, 27 Longford Street, London NW1 3DZ

Printed in Singapore